W9-AQS-890

4/17

LET'S DRAW STEP BY STEP

Let's Draw
Storybook
Characters

Kasia Dudziuk

WINDMILL
BOOKS

Published in 2017 by **Windmill Books**,
an Imprint of Rosen Publishing
29 East 21st Street, New York, NY 10010

Copyright © 2017 Arcturus Holdings Limited

Illustrations: Kasia Dudziuk
Text: JMS Books
Designer: Chris Bell
Editors: Joe Harris and Anna Brett

Cataloging-in-Publication Data
Names: Dudziuk, Kasia.
Title: Let's draw storybook characters / Kasia Dudziuk.
Description: New York : Windmill Books, 2017. | Series: Let's draw step by step | Includes index.
Identifiers: ISBN 9781499481822 (pbk.) | ISBN 9781499481839 (library bound) | ISBN 9781508192916 (6 pack)
Subjects: LCSH: Characters and characteristics in art--Juvenile literature. | Characters and characteristics in literature--Juvenile literature. | Drawing--Technique--Juvenile literature.
Classification: LCC NC825.C43 D83 2017 | DDC 743'.87--dc23

Manufactured in the United States of America
CPSIA Compliance Information: Batch #BW17PK: For Further Information contact Rosen Publishing, New York, New York at 1-800-237-9932

Contents

Let's draw a dragon!

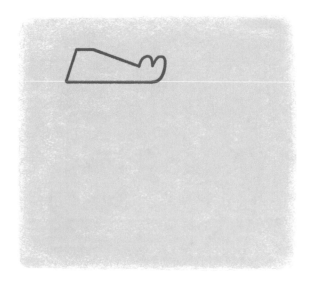

1 Draw the dragon's long head and nose.

2 Give him a body and little ears.

3 Add these shapes for his legs and wings – don't forget his long tail!

4 Draw his face, feet and the spines along his back. Color him in. Does he look fierce?

What about a prince?

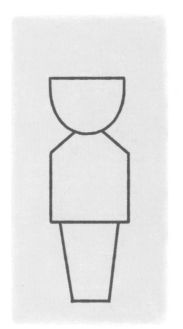

1 Start with the prince's head, body and legs.

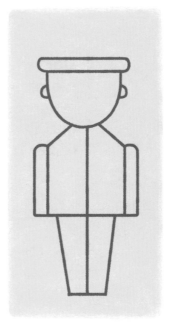

2 Add some more details like this.

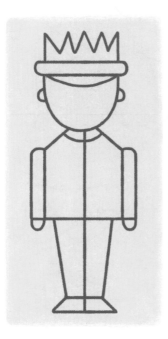

3 Don't forget his hands, feet and crown!

4 Draw his face and the rest of his uniform, and color him in.

Draw a pretty princess.

 **1** Start with the princess's round head and the top of her body.

 **2** She needs a long dress for the ball.

 **3** Draw her pretty hair and her arms.

 **4** Add her crown, face and feet. Now she's ready for the ball!

You can use lots of different colors.

Try drawing a unicorn.

1 First draw an oblong shape for the unicorn's body.

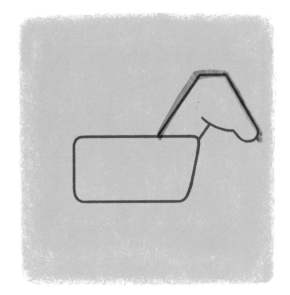

2 Then add his head and neck.

3 He needs ears and long graceful legs.

4 He has a shiny horn and a long swishy tail!

Let's try a brave knight.

1 Let's start with the knight's helmet.

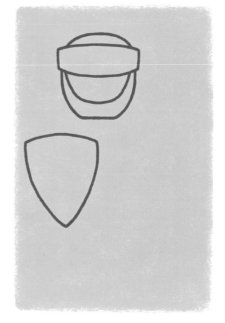

2 He needs a shield.

3 Draw his shiny armor.

4 Add his face, legs and a sharp sword!

Can you draw a wizard?

1 The wizard has a tall pointed hat...

2 ...little ears and a long pointed beard!

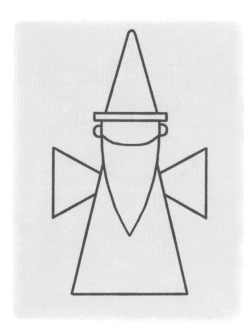

3 Draw his long robe.

4 Add his face, arms and magic wand. Cover him with moons and stars!

Draw a magical fairy.

1 First draw the fairy's head and dress.

2 Now draw her hair.

3 Every fairy needs legs and wings, of course!

4 Add her arms and don't forget her wand! Color her in.

Let's draw a big giant!

1 Begin with the giant's round head and his oblong body.

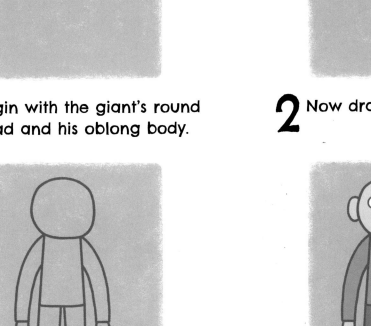

2 Now draw his arms.

3 Give him ragged pants and bare feet, and add his hands.

4 Draw his face and ears, and finish his shirt and pants. Add some trees to show how big he is.

Try drawing Puss in Boots.

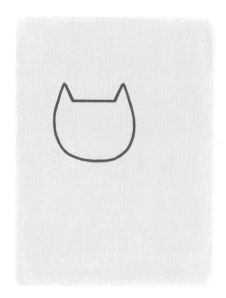

1 First draw this shape for his head and ears.

2 Now draw his body and arms.

3 He needs a fluffy tail, a nice hat and his boots, of course!

4 Draw his face and put a feather in his hat. Color his hat black, his boots brown and his fur orange.

Draw a fairy godmother!

1 First draw this shape for her head and hair.

2 Add her pointed hat and two circles under her head.

3 Now draw her arms and finish her dress.

4 Add her face and legs. She also needs wings and a magic wand, of course!

Learn to draw a genie.

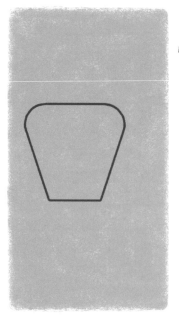

1 Start with this shape for the genie's body.

2 Add his face at the top and his wispy tail at the bottom.

3 Draw a jewel in the center of his turban. His arms are folded.

4 Finish his turban, add a belt and cuffs on his arms. He has a happy face.

Can you draw a lamp for your genie?

How about a mermaid?

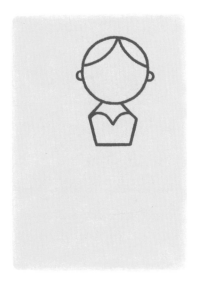

1 Start with her head and the top of her outfit. She has bangs.

2 Next draw her long flowing hair, and her arms and hands.

3 She has a beautiful long tail!

4 Draw her face and some scales on her tail. Color her in.

Draw Little Red Riding Hood.

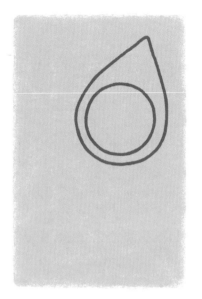

1 Start by drawing the pointed hood around her face.

2 Now draw her coat and arms.

3 Add her legs and boots. She needs a basket to take to Grandma's.

4 Draw her face and hair, and finish off her coat. Her outfit should be bright red, of course!

Now try the Big Bad Wolf!

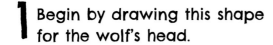

1 Begin by drawing this shape for the wolf's head.

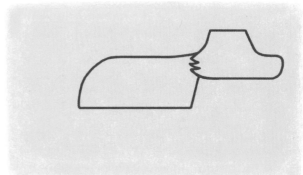

2 Now draw his body.

3 He needs four long legs.

4 Add his bushy tail, face and ears. Color him gray.

Can you draw Dracula?

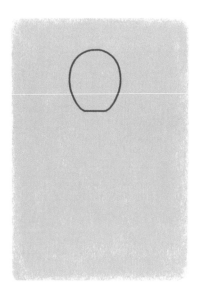

1 Start with Dracula's head. Make it flat at the bottom.

2 Draw a square for his body and his high collar.

3 Add his legs and feet. His arms point upwards.

4 Draw his face, hair and cloak. Don't forget his fangs! Color him black, purple and red.

What about a witch?

1 Start with her head and body. Her dress is a triangular shape.

2 Add her arms, hair and ears. She needs a brim for her witch's hat!

3 Finish her hair and pointed hat. Draw her legs and feet, and a broomstick in her hand.

4 Draw her face and finish her broomstick. Color her in.

Witches fly on their broomsticks like this.

19

Learn to draw a troll.

1 To start, draw a circle for the troll's head.

2 Then draw his big ears and the top part of his body.

3 Add his big ugly nose, and draw his arms, legs and belt.

4 Give him some hair and color him in a ghastly shade of green, with brown pants and a black belt!

You can give your trolls different hairstyles!

Draw Frankenstein's monster.

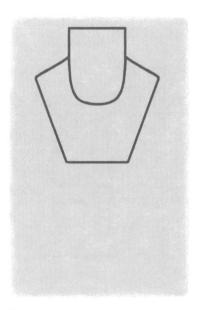

1 Start with these shapes for his head and body.

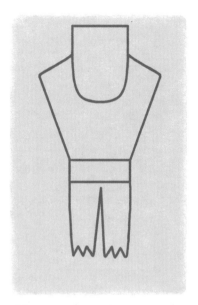

2 Now draw his belt and ragged pants.

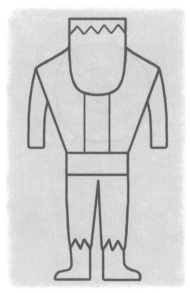

3 Add his arms and feet. Draw his hair and the edges of his coat.

4 Draw his face and hands and color him in. Don't forget the bolts in his neck!

Let's draw a mummy!

1 First draw his head and body. His head is big and round.

2 Now draw his legs and feet.

3 Add the opening for his eyes, and his arms, with a bit of bandage hanging off!

4 Finish all his bandages like this and draw his eyes. Color his face green!

Try drawing a robot.

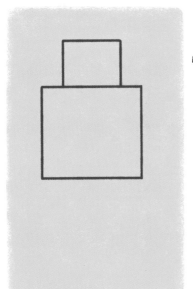

1 The robot's head and body are two squares.

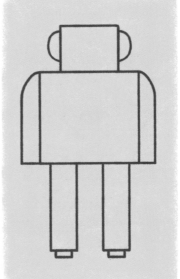

2 Draw his arms, legs and ears.

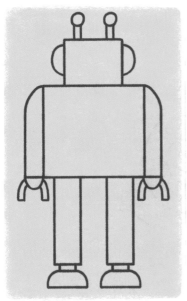

3 Add his hands, two antennae and feet.

4 Add his face and lots of robot details, such as colored lights and a dial on his tummy.

You can draw more robots using different shapes and colors.

What about an alien?

1 The alien has a circle for his head.

2 Now draw his body.

3 Add his little arms, legs and feet.

4 He only has one big eye! Color your little alien green.

You can change the way your alien looks.

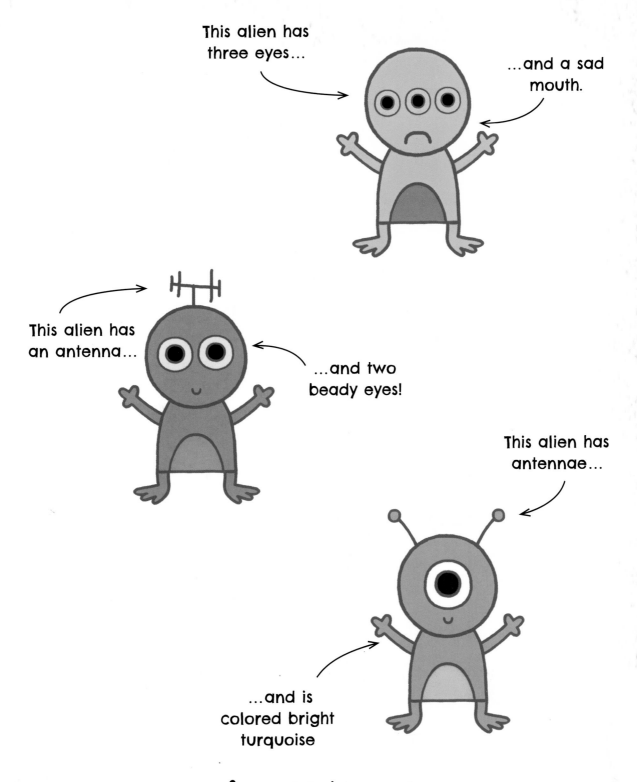

This alien has three eyes...

...and a sad mouth.

This alien has an antenna...

...and two beady eyes!

This alien has antennae...

...and is colored bright turquoise

Can you think of more ways to draw an alien?

How about a snowman?

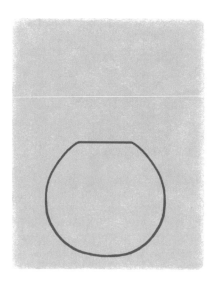

1 First draw a round shape for his body...

2 ...and a smaller round shape for his head. Add the brim of his hat and a scarf.

3 Draw the top of his hat. Add his carrot nose and the ends of his scarf.

4 Finish by adding his face, some nice buttons and twiggy arms. Color him in.

Learn to draw an elf.

1 Start with his head. Add some hair and his big pointed ears.

2 Draw his clothes, an arm and his legs.

3 He needs a hat with a bell and elf boots. Draw a square for his present.

4 Add his smiley face and a belt. Draw a ribbon on his present. Color him in – don't forget his stripy socks!

Learn to draw Santa.

1 First draw his head. He has a long beard, and a small nose and ears. Add the fur around his hat.

2 Now finish off his hat and draw the top half of his body.

3 Draw his tummy and legs. His arms are open wide!

4 Add his face, belt and boots. Color him in – his outfit is red with white fur around the edge and his mittens are green.

Now draw Mrs. Claus!

1 Start by drawing her head, hair and ears.

2 Draw her dress, with fur at the bottom and around her hat. Draw her bun.

3 Complete her hat and add her arms, legs and feet.

4 Finish off her outfit and draw her face. Color her in.

Glossary

alien A being from another planet.

antennae Two long, thin body parts on the heads of insects and other creatures, used to feel and smell.

armor A metal covering that protects soldiers such as knights when fighting.

Dracula A famous vampire in a story written by Bram Stoker.

Frankenstein's monster A monster made by Dr. Frankenstein in a scary story by Mary Shelley.

genie A magic spirit in storybooks that lives in a lamp.

helmet A hard hat that protects the head.

troll A monster in stories that lives in caves and under bridges.

turban A long scarf that is wrapped around the head.

unicorn A horse from storybooks that has a long horn on its forehead.

wizard A person who is very good at magic or has magical powers.

Further reading

How to Draw 101 Princess Things by Barry Green (Top That Publishing, 2014)

How to Draw 101 Really Cute Characters by Barry Green (Top That Publishing, 2014)

How to Draw Princesses and Ballerinas by Fiona Watt (Usborne Publishing Ltd, 2013)

It's Fun to Draw Dinosaurs and Other Prehistoric Creatures (Sky Pony Press, 2011)

Step-by-Step Drawing People by Fiona Watt (Usborne Publishing Ltd, 2014)

Watch Me Draw a Magical Fairy World (Walter Foster Library, 2010)

Websites

For web resources related to the subject of this book, go to:
www.windmillbooks.com/weblinks and select this book's title.

Index